TONY ROBINS ▲ BRIGITTE SHIM ▼ THOMAS SYMONS

edited by **ADELE WEDER**

ron thom
AND THE ALLIED ARTS

WEST VANCOUVER MUSEUM

CONTENTS

FOREWORD

RON THOM AND THE ALLIED ARTS is the result of an unprecedented collaboration between Trent University, Massey College, the Canadian Architectural Archives in Calgary, and the West Vancouver Museum, with each institution contributing its own expertise, resources and archival materials.

Organized by independent curator Adele Weder, this exhibition and catalogue arrives at a propitious moment, as Massey College and Trent University mark their 50th anniversaries in 2013 and 2014. They are rightly proud of their internationally renowned Ron Thom architecture and aware of their responsibility to maintain it for the ages. From our perspective on the west coast, we also have good reason to celebrate. For Ron Thom, British Columbia was both training ground and laboratory. He brought with him to Ontario his deep love and appreciation of nature that would infuse both Massey and Trent, connecting these faraway regions of Canada in a rare and powerful way. Part of the mandate of the West Vancouver Museum is to advance our understanding of the architectural spirit that informed these projects.

There are now more people than ever who appreciate the values and aesthetics of midcentury modernism. Vancouver's north shore has been the hothouse for much of this, with B.C. Binning, Arthur Erickson, Peter Oberlander, Abraham Rogatnik and of course Ron Thom helping define the movement through their writings, teachings and architecture. Those cultural leaders are now gone, and much of their architecture is demolished or at risk. If we do not explore and celebrate their accomplishments now, we risk losing our collective memory of them.

As director/curator of the West Vancouver Museum, I can affirm we are proud to be the inaugural host and full partner in this endeavour. We are deeply grateful to Shanna Fromson, who had the privilege of working with Ron Thom, and whose generous support has made this catalogue possible. ▲

DARRIN MORRISON

v

< Ron Thom, c. 1962
Photographer unknown

ron thom and the allied arts

RON THOM was a man of many talents and, although architecture emerged as the dominant one, he retained a lifelong appreciation for all cultural production. Born in 1923 in Penticton, British Columbia, he moved to Vancouver with his family at age nine and seemed predestined for a career in the arts. A precocious pianist from childhood through adolescence, Thom then switched to the study and practice of visual art, and from there to architecture, which remained his lifelong passion and vocation. But Thom never attended architecture school. Instead, he took advantage of the Canadian government's war-service education subsidy to study at the Vancouver School of Art. He worked briefly as a visual artist before a multi-year apprenticeship with Sharp & Thompson, Berwick, Pratt, Vancouver's largest and most important architectural firm of the day. Upon Thornton Sharp's retirement, the firm became known as Thompson, Berwick & Pratt, and continued to dominate the city's architectural industry and train its best practitioners.

At TB&P, Thom worked closely with Ned Pratt, the principal designer of many of the firm's larger works; and Bob Berwick, a managing architect. He also drew inspiration and instruction from an exceptional group of peers including Dick Mann, Bob Burniston, Bob Boal, Dick Archimbault and Barry Downs. Dick Sai-Chew became a trusted collaborator and would eventually rejoin him in Ontario to work on Trent University. Fred Hollingsworth, a high-school classmate of Ron's, became a lifelong close friend. After-hours, Ron Thom worked with these and other architects designing dozens of

> Detail drawings of gutter and roof, Case House, 1965.

>> Ceramic Vase, Shoji Hamada, gift from the artist to
Ron Thom, 1972. *Photo: Ken Dyke. Collection of the Thom family.*

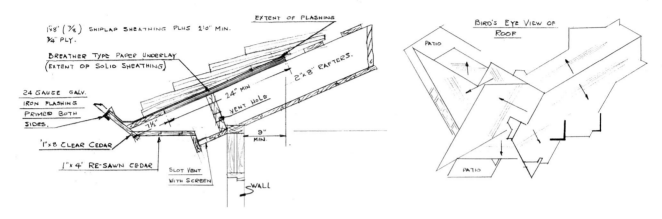

SKETCH OF EAVES & GUTTERS

1'x8' (⅞) SHIPLAP SHEATHING PLUS 2'0" MIN. ¾" PLY.

EXTENT OF FLASHING

BREATHER TYPE PAPER UNDERLAY (EXTENT OF SOLID SHEATHING)

2"x8" RAFTERS.

24 GAUGE GALV. IRON FLASHING PRIMED BOTH SIDES.

24" MIN. VENT HOLE

7½"

9" MIN.

'1"x8 CLEAR CEDAR

1"x 4' RE-SAWN CEDAR

SLOT VENT WITH SCREEN

WALL

BIRD'S EYE VIEW OF ROOF

PATIO

PATIO

gracefully proportioned modular houses, which became informally known as "2 a.m. specials" for the moonlighting schedule of their creators. But Thom also began designing more heavily individualized custom homes, many of which would later be recognized as landmarks. Among others, these include the Ames, Cohen, Narod, Jarvis, Rogers-Dumaresq and Segal houses in Vancouver; the Trier-Pevecz and Boyd-McPhedran Houses in West Vancouver; the Mayhew residence in Victoria, and others. During a career that spanned almost four decades, he and his associates designed iconic projects across the country, including the B.C. Electric Building in downtown Vancouver (converted in 1992 into the Electra condominium tower); Sir Sandford Fleming College in Peterborough; Queen's University Metropolitan Toronto Zoo, Shaw Festival Theatre in Niagara-on-the-Lake; Pearson College of the Pacific on Vancouver Island; the Prince Hotel and Atria Building in Toronto, and many more significant homes in British

Columbia and Ontario, including the Frum and Fraser residences in Toronto.

Throughout his life and work, Thom retained his devotion to the landscape enveloping his architecture and fittings within it. He absorbed and retained love of British collegiate architecture and of Japanese art and design. He respected and conferred with builders, craftsmen and potters. One of his most cherished possessions was a vase given to him by Shoji Hamada in 1972. Thom visited the renowned ceramic artist's studio in Japan during a research trip prior to designing the Prince Hotel in Toronto. Hamada personally invited Thom to select a vase from his shelf of "seconds," pieces with slight variations or flaws, which made them imperfect—or unique, depending on one's perspective. In this particular Hamada vase, we can glimpse a catalogue of Thom's fundamental aesthetic values: earthy red and brown tones, jacknife angle, jagged dark outlines and the hexagonal shape of the vessel itself.

Ron Thom's proclivities lay with the Mingei, or folk craft, movement of which Hamada was a leader, wherein potters and other artisans worked outside of the dominant industrial culture of the age and found a higher level of beauty in that which had been rendered by hand. Whether in the rough-cut cedar of a budget bungalow or the one-off ceramics commissioned for a star client, Thom preferred artful irregularity to machine-like precision or the sterile white purity of Le Corbusier and his professional descendents. Craftwork of all genres and scales informed and inspired Ron Thom's architecture, befitting an age that celebrated the concept of the allied arts, wherein the fields of architecture, visual art, ceramics, furniture and landscape design formed a continuum. He designed more than a hundred houses in the Vancouver region over a large spectrum of construction budgets, but whenever possible with slavish attention to the artisan character of the structure, to the contents inside and landscape around it, and to the larger purpose of advancing architecture into a different realm: not above the other arts but a part of them.

Ron Thom and the Allied Arts is not a retrospective of Thom's full and broad career but a focused exploration of certain works that embody his west-coast provenance and devotion to the allied arts. The architecture featured in these pages—the Copp, Carmichael, Dodek, Forrest and Case houses of the Vancouver region, and Massey College and Trent University in Ontario— are landmark projects that bespeak his ethos with particular clarity. Roughly a half-century after their constructions, these university buildings and five houses continue to serve their original purposes, sheltering their inhabitants and delighting the eye: a testament to the enduring value of the art of architecture. ▲

ADELE WEDER
Curator | *Ron Thom and the Allied Arts* 3

emerging artist, emerging architect

RON THOM attended the Vancouver School of Art from 1942 to 1947, a time of transition and upheaval. Because of the ongoing war, the student body was small, with attendence interrupted by military service. But director Charles H. Scott enlisted several teachers of powerful talent and influence, including Jack Shadbolt, Fred Amess and B.C. Binning. Many of Thom's fellow students—who included Gordon Smith, Don Jarvis, Rudy Kovach, Peter Aspell, Bruno Bobak and Christine Millard— became crucial friends and colleagues. Millard, a multidisciplinary artist and talented potter, would soon become Chris Thom, his first wife. Kovach would later work as Thom's graphic designer and communications consultant. Bruno Bobak and Molly Lamb, who would later marry,

met Thom at the school and remained close and influential friends for life. Molly Lamb Bobak would later remember Charles Scott's studio as detached and stuffy; Shadbolt's arrival marked a seismic shift in tone and approach. Shadbolt eschewed the neoclassical painting that had previously dominated the curriculum, and endorsed a fiercely contemporary form of expression. Shadbolt saw an emerging talent in Ron Thom, and, in a 1946 article in *Canadian Art*, singled him out as one of the emerging artists to watch, who—along with Peter Aspell, Don Jarvis and Rudy Kovach, "will bring a new paradigm to contemporary painting," he predicted.[1] Though Shadbolt would remain a trusted colleague throughtout Thom's life, it was Bert Binning who had the more direct life-changing influence

1 Jack Shadbolt, "A Report on Art Today in British Columbia," *Canadian Art*, Nov. 1946, p. 4.

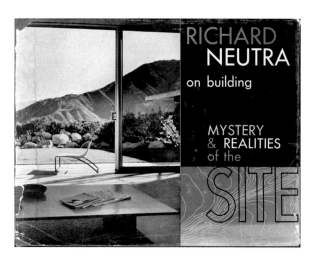

upon him. Binning, an *architect manqué* who would later become recognized as one of Canada's most important painters, taught a course in architectural drawing. Binning recognized the emerging design talent in Thom, and persuaded him to switch career paths from art to architecture. Thom then began his apprenticeship at Sharp & Thompson, Berwick, Pratt. While Ron Thom focused on his burgeoning career, his new wife Chris was largely house-bound, her artistic production suddenly limited to the creation of intricate ceramic beads, which she crafted and fired in the fleeting moments between household duties, and which were later made into necklaces, curtains and room dividers for clients, family and friends.

Working under Ned Pratt, Thom quickly became known as the firm's top draftsman and a rising star. Along with close friend and colleague Fred Hollingsworth, Thom developed a strong taste for the works of Frank Lloyd Wright, which were widely published in books and journals of the day. In 1949, he met Richard Neutra when his former teacher Bert Binning invited the Austrian-born, California-based architect to Vancouver for a public lecture. Neutra's call for the integration of architecture and site made a deep impact upon Thom. Still, it was more

often artists—rather than architects—whom Thom would credit as mentors. "Binning taught me to see, and he taught me to think," Thom later recounted. "The strongest thing he taught us, which has had a profound influence on everything I've done in architecture since, was that every aspect of the design had to respond directly to the world around it, whether it be colour or form, or where the light came in, or the views looking out." The correlation between Ron Thom's brief career in visual art and his later

work in architecture is subtle but undeniable. His compositions were centrifugally arranged, drawn towards the centre, and with strong articulating lines—an approach that he would embrace for his architecture as well. One of the more explicitly comparable examples is the interior of his 1962 Forrest House, as photographed by Selwyn Pullan; and his 1947 oil painting entitled *Seated Figure*. The thick, dark, strongly oblique organizing lines of the painting echo those of the Forrest House central hallway, pulling the viewer into the centre and affirming a highly inward-looking perspective. ▲

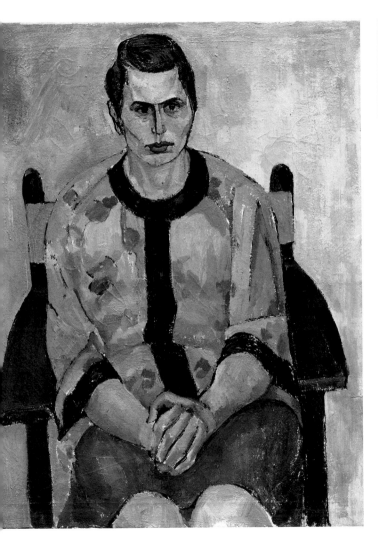

Ceramic beads, by Chris Thom, c. 1949–1960. *Photo: Josh Nychuk. Collections of the Copp and Thom families.*

Seated Figure (adjusted to black-and-white), Ron Thom, 1947. *Collection of the Vancouver Art Gallery.*

Forrest House interior, Ron Thom, 1962. *Photo: Selwyn Pullan.*

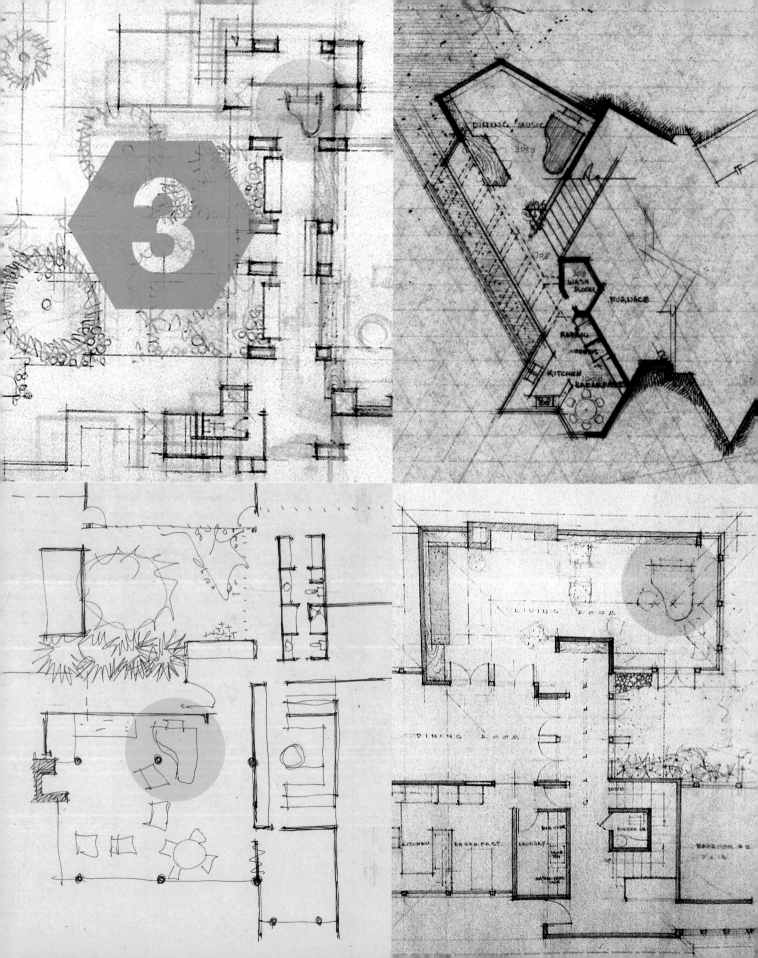

a foundation in music

GROWING UP, Ron Thom had a different career charted out for him: concert pianist. For years, he practised several hours a day, progressing through the rigorous program of the Toronto Conservatory of Music, and winning or placing in provincial competitions. In his late teens, Thom dropped his musical ambitions, switched the study of visual art, and essentially never played the piano in public again. Yet his love of music was literally inscribed in his work: a surprising number of his house sketches present the distinctive outlines of a grand piano, as though it were as much a part of the architecture as the supporting walls. The plan for the Flader House in North Vancouver shows his careful diagrammatic of how the light would fall through the windows upon the instrument. A plan for the unbuilt LaCharity House in Ottawa shows the grand piano at the nucleus of the house, with a processional hallway leading up to the instrument in its sequestered space. The Case House piano is sketched in with the same visual permanence as its built-in trapezoidal table. Thom occasionally endorsed a "piano space" even for clients who didn't own or play the instrument. Though architecture remained his life's work and the focus of his conscious attention, music remained an implicit reference point for much of his worldview. As he once wrote to his former art teacher, Jack Shadbolt: "One of the things that I enjoy thinking about are the periods in history, such as the age of J.S. Bach, when a man's beliefs about his art were at one with his beliefs about the world at large." ▲

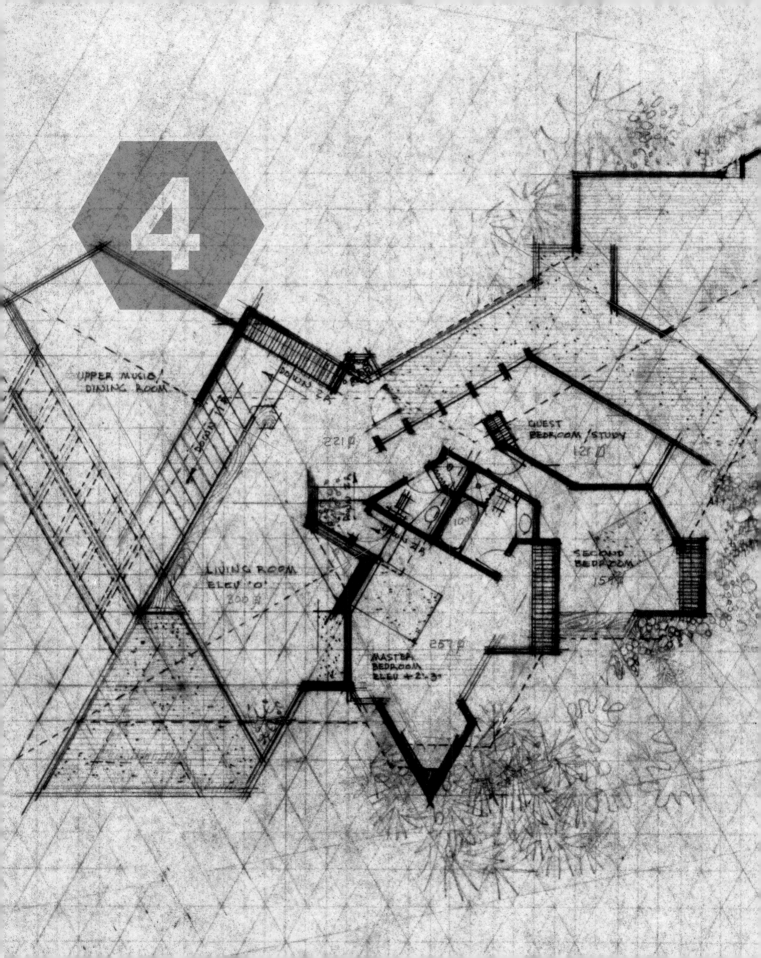

bending space

RON THOM often veered away from the conventional orthogonal grid to explore different modes of configuring form and space. He occasionally laid out his plans on a diamond-shaped grid, which allowed him to create dramatically shaped structures with taut mathematical logic. For this, he looked closely at Frank Lloyd Wright's series of diamond module houses, which defied the monotony of predictable rectilinear houses. The architect would begin by drawing a set of parallel lines and then intersecting them with diagonal lines to create a matrix of diamond-shaped units that could each be reduced to two triangular units, or conflated into larger polygon-shaped units. In what was likely a nod to Wright's 1936 Hanna House, Thom devised his Carmichael House in West Vancouver as a honeycomb of hexagonal modules that generate a sequence of uncanny spaces and angles, which are echoed in the furniture legs, desk drawers, countertops and front door of the house. The hex module system also allowed the architect more possibilities to configure space vertically; the Carmichael House—like the Hanna House—is distinguished by sudden and impressive expansions in ceiling height that foster the sense of space unfolding in all three directions as one walks through the house. Thom used variations of the diamond grid for the ceilings of the Round Room at Massey College and the dining hall at Trent University's Champlain College. The diamond grid is also the form-generator of the Rose Crescent houses and the 1965 Case House, all in West

> Front door, Carmichael House. *Photo: Josh Nychuk.*
Collection of Jan Pidhirny and Jim Ferguson.

∨ Desk drawers, Carmichael House. *Photo: Josh Nychuk.*
Collection of Jan Pidhirny and Jim Ferguson.

>> Elevations and floor plans, Carmichael House.

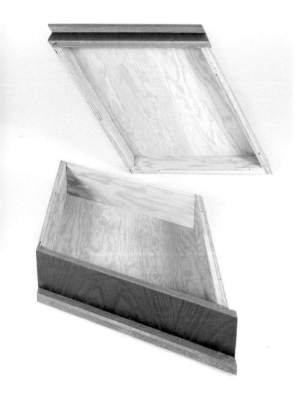

14

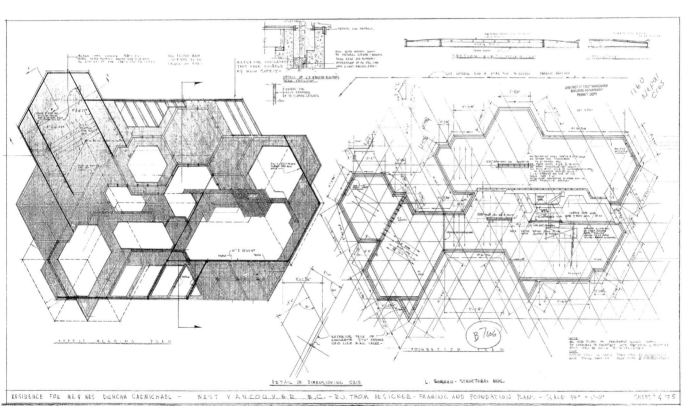

RESIDENCE FOR MR & MRS DUNCAN CARMICHAEL — WEST VANCOUVER B.C. — R.J. THOM DESIGNER — FRAMING AND FOUNDATION PLANS — SCALE: ¼" = 1'-0"   SHEET # 4 '75

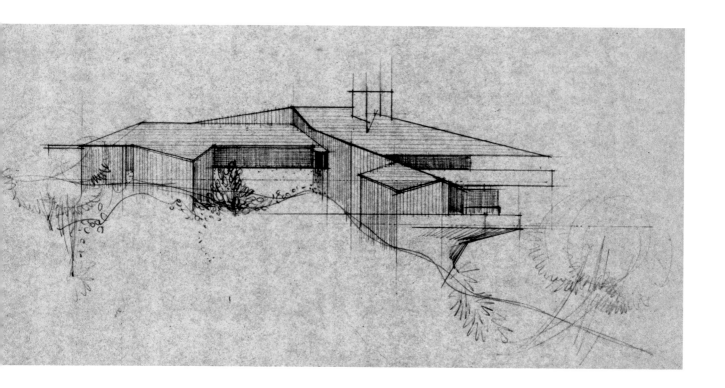

Vancouver. Most of the corners in these houses boast angles of 30, 60 or 120 degrees rather than the 90-degree standard. The obtuse and acute angles generate a sequence of trapezoidal built-in tabletops, shelving, banquettes, stairway, window mullions, and even some of the standalone furniture. The resulting sightlines and spatial complexities imbue these projects with a distinctive and at times unsettling dynamic. Thom worked with clients Dennis and Adele Case to design their built-in dining-table and free-standing matching bench to follow the matrix of the diamond-grid house plan, which generates its unusual angles. Even the stairway and window mullions of the Case House follow the oblique grid of the plan. "A house should have character and individuality, and if possible an air of mystery," wrote the Cases in a 1963 letter to Ron Thom. "Perhaps you will agree that angles promote the greatest interest and mystery."[1] The cost of building this way was far more expensive than conventional design and construction: as the Cases eventually conceded, it required much more "thinking time" from the contractor. ▲

1 Thomson Berwick & Pratt fonds, Canadian Architectural Archives, University of Calgary.

< Wooden bench, Case House. *Collection of Ed and Edlyn Pattyn.*

∨ Plan for built-in table, Case House. *Collection of the West Vancouver Museum.*

∨∨ Drawings for window details, Case House. *Collection of the West Vancouver Museum.*

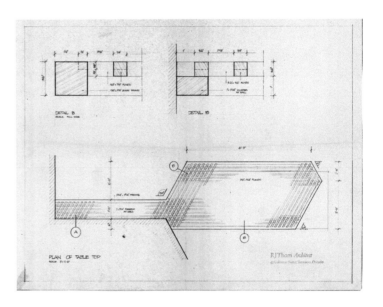

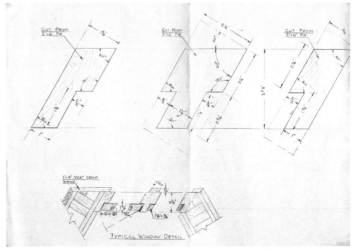

tony robins

BEYOND A FORMIDABLE SHADOW
Observations on Thom's West Coast Spatial Mastery

THERE'S A DISCREET, shared acknowledgement surrounding Ron Thom's architecture: a silence, followed by a nod or a headshake, accepting and forgiving the massive presence of Frank Lloyd Wright. Wright's work was a prime resource for so many North American architects in the first half of the last century, mostly because he was brilliant, but also because his style was both uniquely American and seductively holistic in its incorporation of every visual element. Like many European movements around the turn of the century, he imbued everything with his style, from custom-designed chairs and light fixtures to cutlery and concrete blocks. For Thom, Wright served as great influence in his early years coming up to speed as an architect with no formal architectural education—remarkably, like Wright's own self-taught career.

Standing in those very large shoes, Thom joined a nationwide group of followers that included his contemporary and chief "competitor," Arthur Erickson. It was, I believe, a grand training and a valid one. Music students compose in the style of Beethoven and Mozart to understand masterful composition, to grasp the "rules," and only then go on to break them in a personal way. Looking at many of the world's leading architects, one sees similar paths that springboarded them to great things. As a result, however, North America is littered with half-baked versions of Le Corbusier's La Tourette Monastery, Mies van der Rohe's Seagram Building and the like. Thom implicitly defended this approach, in his observation that "Every child learns by imitation."[1] It takes at least half a career to establish one's own architecture, and most (of us) never really achieve this.

1 Douglas Shadbolt, *Ron Thom: The Shaping of an Architect* (Douglas & McIntyre: 1995), 43.

The necessary step, then, is to jump from imitation to meaningful appropriation. "Good artists copy, great artists steal" is a phrase variously attributed to Picasso, T.S. Eliot, Faulkner and Stravinsky. It describes the necessary step up to establishing a unique voice in any art form. Usually this is achieved by a "mash up" of several influences, like fusion cuisine creating a new taste. In film, Quentin Tarantino references many actual moments from his favourite movies, considered "homage," and clever, because the resultant montage is undeniably his own. The audience becomes part of the game too, enjoyably spotting the multiple references. For Ron Thom, the compilation was a mixture of Wright with a sprinkling of Neutra and some Schindler, along with all of their profound Japanese roots.

Ron Thom swung from letting his guard down by replicating Wright—I think here of the Carmichael House floor plan, or the truly lovely but derivative precast concrete blocks for the Boyd House fireplace—to excelling at using Wright as a starting point to something new. Where he really stands out is in appropriating *spatial devices*, in a way that moved on from matching Wright's implementation of them. Although I am not a Thom scholar, I can speak to architectural space. At architecture school in England, I looked at the effect of wall mass on

spatial experience, learning from my own mentor Richard Padovan, who had discovered the Dutch monk van der Laan and translated his writings on spatial insights. More recently, at the University of British Columbia School of Architecture, I have been teaching an annual studio exploring architectural space. I have catalogued twenty-six techniques, a tool-kit of ways to manipulate the spatial envelope: the walls, floor and ceiling that create space. I'd like to reveal several of Thom's spatial techniques—both absorbed from Wright and developed further—that I believe contribute greatly to our reverence of his work.

Wright's penchant for spatial "compression and expansion" was a clear influence on Thom. The idea is to lower the ceiling of, for example, an entry space in order to reinforce the delight of higher volumes elsewhere. In much the same way, a song does not begin with the chorus, but acclimatises the audience to a more minimal sound, thus creating a far greater effect when the full choir kicks in. Wright scaled spaces to his own stature in the first place, resulting in his standard ceiling height of only 7'6". When downsizing *that*, he succeeded in a really apparent compression of space. My hair virtually brushed the ceiling of the entry area of Wright's Robie House, and I intuitively ducked entering his church lobby in Kansas City. Thom uses this

effectively in the Dodek House. The blunt, low and confined entry room demands an axial twist as one perceives the relief of the living room to the left and its intrigue of spatial height variations and textures beyond, drawing one in as the light begins to reveal the space above and beyond, out of the shadow.

A second technique is to play "dark against light," often introducing daylight into a room in an unusual way to enhance this contrast. It ties contextually to a forest experience (Case and Boyd House) and in some cases (Dodek and Works/Baker House) to the garden immediately outside: the Japanese-influenced play of light on leaves, of one's constant viewing of patches of strong light piercing the canopy and dark low spots one has to work at to understand.

Wright—and then Thom—introduced light selectively at the ceiling level as long thin window bands, bringing one's eye upward to note the ceiling plane. Otherwise, a ceiling normally more or less disappears above one's vision. Thom had no fear of dark corners— all the better for the drama of the overall volume, providing formidable shadows of the real kind. Some homeowners have felt compelled to add windows or incorporate a ridge skylight; to quote one occupant: "dark and moody is not so easy to live with!" My first thought was that these dark interior patches had been a mistake: an inexperienced architect not getting it right! That was naïve, I later realized; what happens when there are dark corners is that one's eyes adjust to the space gradually. On this principal, Sigurd Lewerentz designed an entire brick church in Sweden, a dimly lit but superb structure that allows one's experience of the space to fill in as the eye slowly begins to put the pieces together. One sequentially sees things not immediately apparent, and I found this ploy a delightful experience in the Dodek House. Wide roof overhangs limit the bleaching of the space through all of that glass, and the brick fireplace sits there in the dim light like an old silent man in a chair waiting for you to notice him.

This leads to a third technique: "spatial ambiguity." Here, Ron Thom began to move away from Wright's hold. He sometimes combined the high windows with beams flying though the spaces so that there is a whole other volume of space above them, a lofty and curious, spatially ambiguous, other world up there. The unclear definition of the room, such as the Copp House living room, immediately makes the room feel more spacious than dimensions might attest. The often non-palatial homes feel expansive. No single wall seems to define the room, and one is left wondering how far the space actually stretches beyond what is immediately visible, as one looks diagonally up through layers of spatial events. Suddenly there is light coming in unexpectedly, way up in a corner, to ensure the height and drama is truly felt.

Ron Thom's fourth spatial gesture was to incorporate surreally large-scale fireplaces, probably inspired straight from Wright. But unlike his mentor, Thom contrasted the massive hearth with a generally ethereal lightness throughout the rest of the building. This touches a few spatial tools: "heavy against light", "tactility" and "materiality." The wood-stud walls, cedar clad both inside and out, the floor-to-ceiling single-glazed windows with butted glass and the thin roof all add to the sense of ephemerality and the delightfully contrasting lack of weight. Cedar is feather-light. One can do harm to it with a fingernail, and its presence everywhere, on ceilings and cabinetry as well as walls, uplifts the room with its fragility: a diminution of room mass against the powerful brick hearths. Here Thom breaks into his stride, managing to refer uniquely to the temporality of the West Coast, from the disappearing relics of the First Nations' buildings and totems, the beautiful rotting trunks within our distant virgin forests, and to the superficiality of Western presence in these regions. The massive fireplaces bring gravitas and a welcome harkening to medieval times, the *weight* —all that history and ancient building—of Europe, to our own thin new city. Doubly, they harken back to campfires of thousands of years of habitation before European contact. They are simply perfect

for Vancouver, a contextual *tour de force* in part because of our subconscious desire to fill that void. They ground the building and, interestingly, they literally provide a seismic, structural grounding too, in our earthquake-prone province.

The most powerful example of this is in the 1957 Carmichael House. It stands as if the whole room is subservient to its power. In 1962 Thom did it again in the Forrest House, taking up the whole wall with stone, in a more 1960s fashion, refining the look into a whole new generation of massive fireplaces. It literally *becomes* the room. The sofas built in along the edges are reminiscent of the stone ledges within old European precedents, where one actually sits inside the hearth. Another moment of delight for me was experiencing, within the Copp House, "the air of immobility that precedes decay"[2] to borrow a

phrase from Martin Amis. The fireplace stands defiantly against the slow demise of its surroundings, the patina of water-stained cedar, leaky single-paned windows, tattered leather chairs, and disintegrating drapes.

A related spatial generator is the effect of the construction process on the space. The interior character of Peter Zumthor's Bruder Klaus Field Chapel, for instance, is defined by how it was built: stacking twelve metre tall logs into a pyramid, pouring concrete on the outside, and setting fire to the timbers. Its blackened, inverted lines of the resultant interior tell of its construction history and the labour that went into it. Ron Thom's enormous brick fireplaces tell of the laying of each brick. We've seen bare brick walls before, but never stacked so monumentally inside Vancouver living rooms. There's a presence, in

2 Martin Amis, *Experience* (2000), Alfred A. Knopf Canada. p. 52.

those spaces, of this labour and care and human interaction with the material. And there was probably time, before TV and the internet, to sit in one's easy chair and appreciate that.

Ron Thom's most unique achievement is perhaps, then, his positioning of these directly inspired spatial moves into an Architecture that suits—and is about—its context: the West Coast landscape. He had significantly stepped out on his own in thinking of space as a contextual referent. The Case House exemplifies this well. Wright's most relevant site-contextual work is the remarkable Kaufmann Residence, Fallingwater, where he used circulation and the curving paths and stairs to hug and reveal the rocky ravine. But when it came to the main interior spaces, he designed them as flat, rectilinear volumes in

contrast to the land. The main cantilevered space gains power from one's sense of hovering over a natural riverbed to the sound of . . . falling water. In the 1965 Case House, Thom instead wrapped his interior spaces over the West Vancouver bedrock, giving one a sense of a forest walk, albeit from kitchen to dining room. The Case House spaces literally cascade down and over the actual granite rock face. Though in fact precisely determined by the Wright-influenced "diamond grid" plan, the seemingly haphazard angling of the ceiling and walls convey a movement that reflects the flow of the land as one might negotiate rocky terrain and cedar canopy. Where they fall apart is only when he visually refers back to Wright's geometries. We see moments when he has lapsed into mere replication—a hexagon here or there—but then has taken off again with unique confinements and openings. I became a Ron Thom fan in that house, and sought out and rooted for the specific moments where he had broken from his mentor.

The Case House shows a freeing of roof form, again reflecting the forest canopy, but a more sophisticated development is the entire roof spectacle of the Forrest House. "Angled or curved against straight" is a spatial play most often implemented on plan, such as by Le Corbusier and Robert Venturi, and dramatically in the Crawford Residence by Morphosis. Highlighting a deviation from the orthogonal is most effectively achieved by Thom, however, in three dimensions: the swooping angles of roofline in the Forrest House. They not only create a sculptural building but directly generate the volume of the interior spaces in the modernist tradition, and—unusual for Thom—in white too! The roof is constructed mostly of a single folding plane defining both exterior and interior, contrasted against the flat surface of the ground. Three of its interlocking roofs read as a flock of Canada geese zooming away. (Sadly, their original "bodies," the vertical deco beam elements affixed along the ridges, have disappeared in recent renovations, and more depressing still is the prospect of potential demolition of this historically priceless home).

These birds in flight were another of Thom's blatant—though maybe not conscious—contextual references to nature.

It is through all of these extraordinary spaces, then, that we see Ron Thom as a man inspired, spellbound, and driven for a long time by persuasive influences. We see how he rode those ideas to new ground in Vancouver, however, by taking existent spatial ideas and fusing them spectacularly with the contextual opportunities of the West Coast, thereby, making them his own. Whilst still living in Vancouver, Thom moved to larger work, and began all over again to grapple with the influence of Wright. It permeated his first scheme for the Massey College competition, which he undertook while still living in Vancouver. The jury, which included architects Geoff Massey and Hart Massey, informed him that he could move on to Round Two but needed to drop that stifling Imperial-Hotel vocabulary. It was, implicitly, a plea for Thom to allow his own immense but latent skills to flourish. He did, and they did, and we should thank the Masseys for helping Thom to establish his rightful place in history. At Massey College, with a unique and fresh design, he utilized many of the spatial tools gleaned from those Vancouver house experiments, this time on a huge scale, and finally moved beyond his master's formidable shadow. ▲

the house as prototype

LIKE MANY architects, Ron Thom used his house commissions as a means of exploring concepts, materials and details that he would later employ in larger projects. The distinctive rooflines, hanging lanterns, and leather drawer pull-handles found in his domestic architecture are echoed throughout Massey College and Trent University. The connections are particularly striking between Massey and the home that he designed for Freddie and Dr. Harold Copp, a prominent medical scientist who moved to Vancouver to head the first Department of Physiology at the University of British Columbia. Built in 1951 on an oceanview site near the university, the house offers an architectural précis of Ron Thom's fundamental design approach. Interlocking beams and planes of unpainted wood, which generate uncanny multi-leveled spaces and high clerestory windows; a lightwell seeps down into a dark space; a path through the darkness leads to a sheet of light at the back of the house. These characteristic gestures contribute to the ethereal ambiance of Thom's houses and institutional projects alike. As Massey College neared completion in 1963, he designed several prototypes for its furniture and lighting, many of which ended up as an inspiration or literal presence in his house projects. The symbiosis between furniture, house and college is profound. Ron Thom designed a series of club chairs and prototype wooden tables for Massey, whose proportions and complex wooden stretchers echo the proportions and interlocking volumes of the Copp House itself. "I do think leather is

the right thing" for the bulk of their living-room furniture, he wrote to Freddie and Harold Copp from Toronto in 1964. "It has been my experience that it is impossible to push the use of one material too far. You may remember how limited in this regard was the common room in Massey College."[1] The rejected prototypes ended up in the Copp family home after its 1964 addition: a fitting tribute for the house that served as a template for much of his work. ▲

1 Letter from Ron Thom to Harold and Freddie Copp, 1964,
   Thompson Berwick & Pratt fonds, Canadian Architectural Archives,
   University of Calgary.

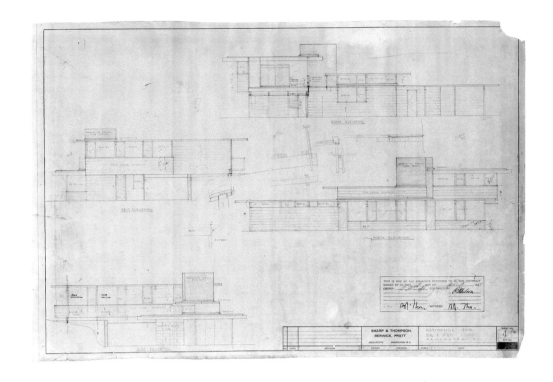

29

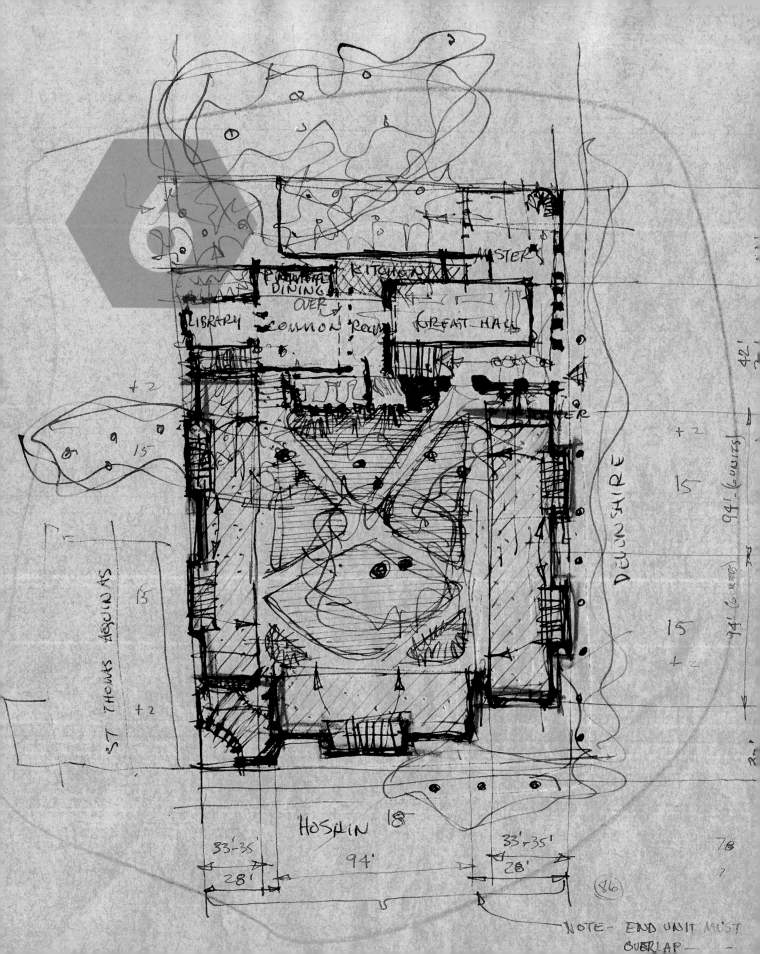

KITCHEN

MASTERS

FORMAL DINING OVER

LIBRARY   COMMON ROOM   GREAT HALL

+2
15

ST THOMAS AQUINAS   15   +2

DEVONSHIRE

+2
15
94' (6 units)
94' (6 units)
42'
15
+2

HOSAIN 18

33'-35'   94'   33'-35'
28'   28'

(86)

78
7

NOTE- END UNIT MUST
OVERLAP—

a total work of art

IN 1960, the Massey Foundation invited Ron Thom and three other prominent architects to submit designs for an exceptional new graduate-student residence in Toronto to be known as Massey College. "It should, in its form, reflect the life that will go on inside it," read the design memorandum, "and should possess certain qualities: dignity, grace, beauty and warmth." The other architects invited to submit proposals for the coveted commission were Arthur Erickson, John Parkin and Carmen Corneil. The Massey College competition embodied Thom's ideal of a *gesamtkunstwerk*, a total work of art into which the architect would design, commission or otherwise oversee each component of the building from the outside in, from the gardens to the ashtrays. Thom made over a hundred preliminary sketches and then a formal Round One presentation in pencil drawings and watercolours, a complex seemingly influenced by Frank Lloyd Wright's Imperial Hotel in Tokyo, and also evocative of some of Thom's finest west coast domestic architecture. These first presentation boards presented a highly decorative scheme with steeply pitched roofs and other Wrightian references, exquisitely rendered by hand. The selection committee, which included Vincent Massey's architect nephew Geoffrey and sons Hart and Lionel, then invited Thom to the final round of the competition, with the proviso that he would rework his earlier scheme. For Round Two, Thom presented a more streamlined, striking flat-roofed design that was nonetheless very craft-centred, and which was enthusiastically accepted by the selection committee.

three common rooms, one of which would be used as a dining room, and a small chapel.

Massey College as a college for graduate students, will be unique in Canada. There is nothing comparable to it in any Canadian university. It is of great importance that it should, in its form, reflect the life which will go on inside it, and should possess certain qualities – dignity, grace, beauty and warmth. Such a college as we have in mind possesses antecedents in various countries, and whatever their physical forms may be or the date of their erection, they have a character in common. What we wish is a home for a community of scholars whose life will have intimacy but at the same time, academic dignity.

34

The Massey College commission changed the course of Thom's career in fundamental ways. It afforded him an unprecedented creative opportunity, generous budget and national profile; and the opportunity to seek the finest craftsmen and ceramic artists. With the help of metalworkers, he devised a series of prototype lanterns and the distinctive iron gate of the College. He enlisted John Reeve to create hundreds of unique ceramic ashtrays and lamps; the British silversmith Eric Clements was selected to design the College's custom silverware. The project also set in motion the impetus for him to uproot from the west coast and move to Toronto. While working on the project, Thom met renowned graphic artist Allan Fleming, who designed the College's coat-of-arms, logo and lettering of the George Santayana quotation[1] that would wrap around the inner perimeter of the dining room, Ondaatje Hall. He also met Fleming's research assistant, Molly

---

1 "Happiness is impossible, and even inconceivable, to a mind without scope and without pause, a mind driven by craving, pleasure or fear. To be happy, you must be reasonable, or you must be tamed. You must have taken the measure of your powers, tasted the fruits of your passion, and learned your place in the world and what things in it can really serve you. To be happy, you must be wise."
—George Santayana

> Prototype for Massey College table lamp,
Ron Thom with Bob Boal (attrib.), c. 1963.
Photo: Ken Dyke. Collection of the Thom family.

∨ Prototype for Massey College lantern,
Ron Thom with Bob Boal (attrib.), c. 1963.
Photo: Ken Dyke. Collection of the Thom family.

>> Massey College, Round Room. *Photo: Peter
Varley. Collection of the Canadian Architectural
Archives at University of Calgary.*

Golby. Thom honed a close friendship with Fleming, and married Golby. In January of 1963 he wrote to his prospective mother-in-law, Betty Golby, that moving from Vancouver to Toronto "would force me to work in a different climate architecturally, one which may be less free in some ways, but altogether more critical. This could be a good thing or a bad thing, depending on me."[2]

Massey College was completed in the fall of 1963 and opened in a momentous ceremony conducted by Vincent Massey and attended by Prince Philip, the Duke of Edinburgh. The building remains in immaculate condition to this day, still serving as a residential community for University of Toronto graduate students. In 2013, the College received the *Prix du xxe siècle* award from the Royal Architectural Institute of Canada and the Heritage Canada Foundation, and the Landmark Award from the Ontario Association of Architects, for its enduring status as a nationally significant architecture landmark. ▲

2 Letter from Ron Thom to Betty Golby, 1963, collection of
   Adam Thom.

brigitte shim

REFLECTIONS ON MASSEY COLLEGE

UPON THE COMPLETION of Massey College in 1963, Founding Master Robertson Davies had deep praise for its designer, Ronald J. Thom. "Our architect has understood our purpose and complemented it architecturally in a way that commands my admiration and gratitude," wrote Davies in *The Canadian Architect*. "On a small site he has contrived a building that combines spaciousness with intimacy."[1] Eric Arthur, an influential University of Toronto academic and the Editorial Advisor to the *Royal Architectural Institute of Canada Journal*, was equally impressed, describing the "recent and generous gift of the Massey Foundation" as "of interest to us as architects, not only for its merits as a building but its means by which the design was achieved."[2] The limited competition involved the four leading architects of the day—Ron Thom, Arthur Erickson, Carmen Corneil and John C.

Parkin. It was a high-profile competition at a exhilarating moment within the architectural profession. Swept away in postwar optimism and yearning for societal transformation, architects weren't just trying to design buildings; they were trying to change the world.

Despite this praise and the unanimity of the selection committee on Ron Thom's final scheme, when Massey College was completed in 1963, it ignited great controversy within architectural circles. "I must confess that there are aspects of the plan that disturb me," wrote James Acland in the October 1963 issue of *Canadian Architect*, "and yet, as an academic, how the building delights me."[3] Perhaps Acland's ambivalence was a reflection of his having a foot in both academic worlds, as a professor of architecture at the University of British Columbia, and a specialist in medieval vaults.

1 Robertson Davies, "Massey College," *Canadian Architect*, Oct. 1963, Vol. 8, No. 10, p. 48.
2 Eric R. Arthur, "Massey College Competition," *Royal Architectural Institute of Canada Journal (RAICJ)*, Dec. 1960.
3 James H. Acland, "Critiques," *Canadian Architect*, Oct. 1963, Vol. 8, No. 10, p. 61.

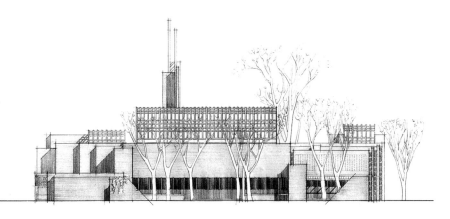

The architect, historian and critic Peter Collins also expressed ambivalence in the October 1963 RAIC *Journal*: "Does Massey College set Canadian architecture back fifty years, as one critic has suggested? The answer can indeed be affirmative; but only if one regards architectural style as comparable to fashions in clothes, whereby the nature of architecture changes every spring."[4] Yet comparing Ron Thom's finished building with the rejected John C. Parkin scheme, Collins noted that Parkin "made a deliberate attempt to utilize and exploit contemporary technology in their design," a key checklist criterion of modernism. The architectural debate at the time, as articulated by Collins, pitted the newly completed Massey College against the International Style work of the Parkin office. For Collins, new technology was inextricably linked to innovation. John C. Parkin's scheme for Massey College's dining hall roof met Collins' modernist criteria: "It exploits the most up-to-date structural system that the spatial requirements of the building will permit."[5]

Then in its heyday, the office of John C. Parkin epitomized the design qualities of the International Style modern movement through the Ortho Pharmaceutical plant and office (1955), Toronto Aeroquay and International Airport (1957–65), and Ottawa Train Station (1966). The firm's signature glass, steel and concrete structures clearly expressed each building's function and program. Its buildings were admired and appreciated locally, nationally and globally. International Style modernism was seen by many architects as the only kind of modernism. But what Ron Thom designed for Massey College didn't fit that mould.

As a building, Massey College was difficult to categorize. Was it "traditional"? It certainly didn't resemble the historic revivalist architecture of E.J. Lennox or John Lyle. Was it "modern"? Perhaps by way of Frank Lloyd Wright, one could argue, but even so—it was peculiar. People wondered: where exactly did it belong on the architectural index?

The evaluations of Massey College, then, were ideologically fraught, with admiration for its beauty tempered by concern over its "traditional" aspects, mixed with bewilderment over its unique and therefore unclassifiable appearance. It did not fit the checklist of modernist architecture: it did not incorporate the estab-

4 Peter Collins, "An Appraisal," RAICJ, (Oct. 1963) Volume XL, No. 10, p. 40.
5 Ibid.

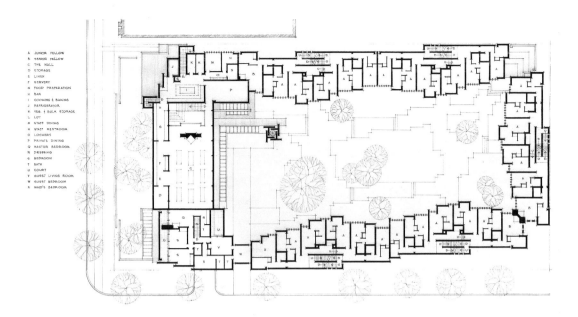

lished material palette; it wasn't white or black or gray; its exterior did not express its internal structure; it had decorative aspects and used brick and limestone and intricate ironwork. The building precisely served the client's purpose, but its construction employed no innovations. Yet it *was* different from traditional neo-classical architecture. In a sense, Massey College became its own paradigm.

From our contemporary perspective, fifty years later, we can link the Massey College project to another groundbreaking project of the same era. In 1958, the international design competition for a New City Hall created a public debate about how the modern movement could link with the city's cultural aspirations. The landmark competition resulted in the New City Hall (1965) by Finnish architect Vijo Revell with John B. Parkin Associates. Its dramatically curvilinear concrete forms projected Toronto as a modern, vibrant metropolis of the future.

It was one of Massey College's early champions, Eric Arthur, who had organized the Toronto City Hall competition. Although entirely different programs, the New City Hall project and Massey College shared the goal of social and cultural transformation within the optimistic climate of postwar Canada: City Hall on a broader public level for the citizenry at large, and Massey College on a selective and intimate level for a small number of scholars.

Ron Thom's first priority for Massey College was the realization of Vincent Massey's vision for a uniquely self-contained student environment, possessing "dignity, grace, beauty and warmth," as the design memorandum explicitly stated. The building would provide study and living accommodations for sixty-eight graduate students; rooms for fifteen senior Fellows and faculty members; a Master's residence; and a dining hall, reading, library and common-room facilities to serve and unite them all.

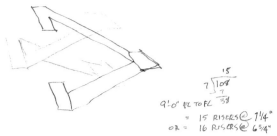

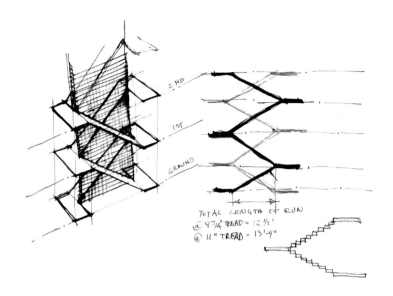

The noisy, constrained urban site called for an inward-looking courtyard. Thom's internal planning of the residence rooms broke down the program into smaller houses, and his clever staircase system defined each smaller community within the larger community. The rooms are communal and yet distinct from one another, meeting the client's broader desire for, "a community of scholars."[6]

The materials list for Massey College was, as Peter Collins noted, "simple—wood, stone, plaster, brick and bronze—and picked with regard to the graceful aging of a building with an anticipated long lifespan, and also with regard to materials possessing intrinsic warmth."[7]

"There is no reason why an architect cannot create a completely contemporary building with a traditional program, traditional materials and geometric forms evolved from an earlier decade," allowed Collins. "But at the same time it does suggest that genuinely epoch-making architecture can only result through the application of the latest technological processes. There is no reason why every building should have to be epoch-making. The trustees of the Massey Foundation did not ask for an epoch-making building. They did ask for a building that would be eminently functional, eminently sturdy and eminently beautiful and that is what they got."[8]

Here, then, the difference: in the spirit of the age, with so many architects trying to challenge their clients, Thom was the only one among the four Massey competitors who had no formal architectural education, having learned about architecture and its allied arts through dialogue, symposia and years of apprenticeship. He was busy trying to understand and collaborate with the clients to realize their vision for a new idea of community that did not yet exist in this country. Both Vincent Massey and Ron Thom fully understood the building not as an end in itself but as a vehicle to enable dialogue between scholars of several generations, resulting in a new community that continues to thrive and flourish to this day—five decades later.

Massey College was largely driven by client forces, but Ron Thom was clearly at home with the materials and language that we traditionally associate with an earlier era. The finials

6 Vincent Massey, "Massey College," RAICJ, Oct. 1963.
7 Collins, RAICJ, Oct. 1963, p. 40.
8 Ibid.

< Massey College stairway system preliminary
  sketch, Ron Thom, 1960. *Collection of the Canadian
  Architectural Archives at University of Calgary.*

∨ Book covers, *Toronto Modern: Architecture
  1945–1965* (left) co-published by BAU and Coach
  House Press, 1987; and second edition (right) with
  new Introduction, co-published by BAU, Coach
  House and APTI, 2002.

atop the gate, like the finials of the otherwise highly modernist 1957 B.C. Electric Building in Vancouver, are—undeniably—ornamental. But Massey is not pretending to be something it's not: empowered by his client, Ron Thom used ornament to create this haven of dignity, grace, beauty and warmth, in effect rendering it as part of the function. Moreover, the nominally ornamental gestures—finials, bas-relief, Allan Fleming's seriffed wall lettering—serve to humanize the scale. Massey College does exemplify social transformation through architecture: not at the global scale that was the obsession of the times, but at the local scale that was the obsession of the client.

As the age of social transformation subsided, our modern heritage became misunderstood, under-appreciated and vulnerable. The 1985 demolition of a modernist cultural landmark— the glass, steel and vitrolite Bulova clocktower on the Canadian National Exhibition Grounds in Toronto—was the catalyst for the formation of the Bureau of Architecture and Urbanism (BAU), of which I was a founding member. As part of a new generation of architects and educators who came of age after this vital time, we sought to raise public awareness through the 1987 exhibition and catalogue *Toronto Modern: Architecture 1945–1965*. The *Toronto Modern* project featured ten exemplary modern buildings which present, as described in the exhibition catalogue, "a capsule history of a formidable generation of new design and construction ideas that flowed through Toronto's urban fabric with the irresistible momentum of electric impulses flowing through circuitry wire."[9] Massey College stands among these ten buildings.

At a time when Post-Modernism's popularity was cresting, we positioned the ten buildings as "case studies for a future inventory of the city's Modern period … a vital mood of expansiveness, experimentation and confidence on the part of architects, their sponsors and their public."[10]

9 Bureau of Architecture and Urbanism, *Toronto Modern: Architecture 1945–1965*. (Toronto: Coach House Press, 1987) p. 5.
10 The ten buildings: 1948 Mechanical Engineering, University of Toronto; 1953 New Town, Don Mills; 1954 Anglo Canadian Insurance Co.; 1955 Ortho Pharmaceuticals, Don Mills; 1955 Benvenuto Place; 1959 Fogel Residence; 1960 O'Keefe Centre; 1963 Massey College; 1963 Toronto-Dominion Centre; 1965 Toronto City Hall.

43

Fittingly, the exhibition *Toronto Modern: Architecture 1945–1965* was held in the Rotunda of the Toronto City Hall.

Massey College is now part of a broader definition of modernism that encompasses not only new materials and structural innovation but their correlative values: sensitivity to its urban context, exemplary craftsmanship and architectural invention. The *Toronto Modern* exhibition catalogue describes Massey College as "a building that is thoroughly Modern in style while observing an extremely sophisticated way the ancient conventions established by St. Anthony's and Nuffield College at Oxford."[11]

The BAU catalogue cites Ron Thom's own edict that the building "should be capable of being seen in many ways and of unfolding itself by degrees—probably never completely." We argued in the *Toronto Modern* catalogue that the college may well be based on British antecedents in terms of its courtyard, but intriguingly combines Dutch-inspired Modernist composition with an attention to detail reminiscent of Frank Lloyd Wright, all of which ultimately fuses into an entirely original and outstanding work of architecture. As the catalogue notes, "The residences are organized around a staircase system, a fact which accounts for the absence of institutional ambience in the building. Materials such as copper flashings and bronze light fixtures have been chosen for their sensual characteristics and for durability, in anticipation of a long life span, but they are detailed in a frankly Modern idiom. Important to the design of the building was the integration of crafts: pottery, calligraphy, silverware and carved stone are part of the architecture, making it an elegant example of the 'total design.'"[12]

With each revisiting of Massey College and its context, our appreciation of modernism grows more nuanced and substantial. In 2002, the original *Toronto Modern* catalogue authors and

11 Bureau of Architecture and Urbanism, *Toronto Modern: Architecture 1945–1965*. (Toronto: Coach House Press, 1987) p. 8.
12 Ibid, p. 68.

BAU co-founders (Marc Baraness, Ruth Cawker, George Kapelos, Detlef Mertins and myself) worked with the Association for Preservation Technology International (APTI) to republish the catalogue for the APTI conference in Toronto that year. In a new preface entitled "Re-Intro-duction," Marco Polo noted that controversy is nothing new. By the time BAU assembled in 1987, wrote Polo, Post-Modernism had reached a zenith with the freshly completed Jones & Kirkland Architect's Mississauga City Hall. At a symposium during the opening events, archi-tect Edward Jones declared that unlike other presenters, he had come not to praise modernism but to bury it. The comments, noted Polo, "were consistent with the view that, contrary to consti-tuting a revolutionary new orthodoxy, Modernism was merely an aberrant temporary interruption of the Western classical tradition."[13]

In 2013, looking back once again on the postwar era, we can clearly see that Modernism has encompassed an expansive range of archi-tectural ideas and, far from an aberration, is enduring well into the 21st century. Its desig-nation under the Ontario Heritage Act, RAIC *Prix du XXe siècle* and Ontario Association of Architects landmark award attest to this. Massey College has indeed remained a community of

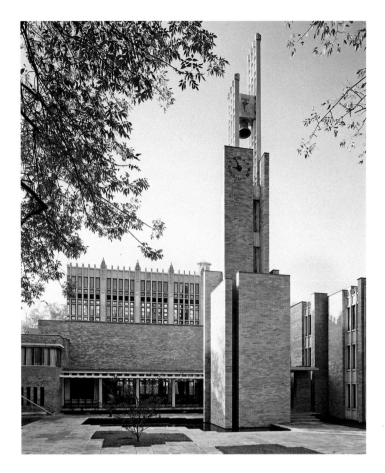

communities, with prominent scholars mingling daily with junior fellows. Informal discussions range from hot political topics to the College limerick writing contest. The distinguished masters of Massey College—from Robertson Davies to Paterson Hume to Anne Saddlemyer and its outgoing Master John Fraser—have each ensured its continuity as a community of scholars.

Let us leave the last word to Founding Master Robertson Davies, who, in concluding his praise for Massey College, observed the following: "A building is unquestionably an influence on the life we live in it, and never more than so [than] when we were young." ▲

13 Marco Polo, "Re-Introduction," *Toronto Modern: Architecture 1945–1965*, Second Edition (Toronto: BAU, Coach House Press and APTI, 2002.) p. ix.

master planner

IN THE late 1950s, a team of visionaries launched the concept for a new liberal arts university in the verdant countryside near Peterborough, Ontario. Team leader Thomas Symons, who was at the time the Dean of Devonshire House at the University of Toronto, happened to pass by the construction site of Massey College every day en route to work. Symons was enraptured by the beauty of that emerging structure, and, upon learning the name of its architect, championed Ron Thom as the master planner and chief architect for what would become Trent University. For Ron Thom, the Trent commission must have seemed a culmination of his life's ambition. Given a generous budget and a picturesque acreage fronting the Otonabee River, Thom would spend much of the next decade

designing or helping oversee *everything*: overall campus plan, roadways, main college buildings, pedestrian paths, landscaping, floor coverings, lighting, desks, cabinets, chairs, tables, stools, dinnerware, artwork, ashtrays. With a mandate that stretched from the transformation of empty fields to the specification of the smallest teaspoon, all while facilitating a more intimate and direct mode of delivering higher education, the Trent University project was one of the most ambitious and comprehensive design commissions in Canadian history.

Ron Thom conceived Trent as a campus set on two opposing riverbanks, with a pedestrian bridge uniting them. That connecting feature—the Reginald Faryon Bridge—would later become an iconic feature of the campus.

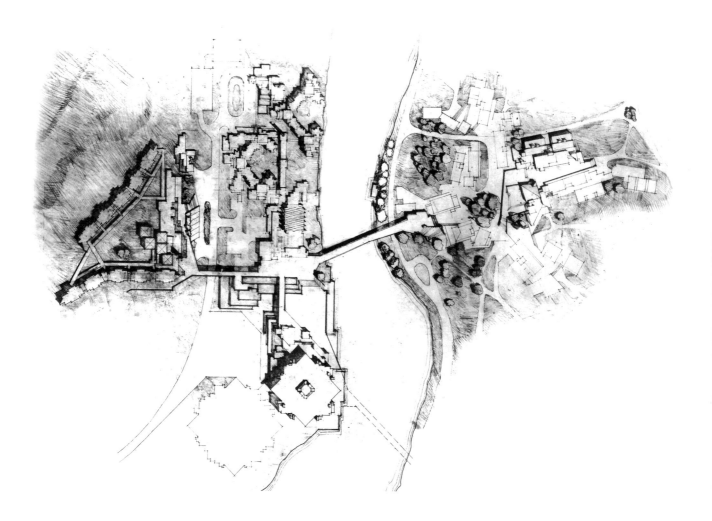

The nascent campus first took form with renovations and expansions of existing Peterborough buildings, which became Catherine Parr Traill College, Peter Robinson College, and Rubidge Hall. Ron Thom then designed the university's flagship building, Champlain College, after a four-week tour of medieval and contemporary colleges in Great Britain. Despite visiting several new universities, he remained most impressed by Oxford and Cambridge universities, whose conscribed courtyards generated a sense of haven and harmony for the students. Inspired by a visit to Eero Saarinen's 1962 Morse and Ezra Stiles

Colleges at Yale University, Thom decided on a rubble-aggregate wall for Champlain, which would become the flagship building and the heart of the campus. The distinctive walls of poured stone and concrete were created in collaboration with engineers Yolles and Bergman. The architects worked closely on the master plan with founding president Symons, vice-president Denis Smith and an advisory group of Trent's board members, future professors and students. The construction process was a mixture of craft and science, and unique at the time: limestone was first placed into the formwork; fly ash was

<< Trent University site plan, rendering by Paul Bernard, Paul Merrick and Alastair Grant, c. 1964.

< Close-up of aggregate-rubble wall, Champlain College, Trent University. *Photo: John Flanders. Collection of the Canadian Architectural Archives at University of Calgary.*

ᴠ Champlain College, Trent University. *Photo: Steven Evans.*

Thom worked with or consigned his senior associates to design Lady Eaton College, the Thomas H. Bata Library, and the Reginald Faryon Bridge. The Trent commission drew on the resources of the firm's gifted designers and staff, including Paul Merrick, Norm Hotson, Alastair Grant, Peter Smith, Bill Lett, Dick Sai-Chew, Robert Montgomery, Paul Martel, Bob McIntyre, Paul Barnard, Daryl Morgan; engineers Ted Crossey, Roly Bergmann and Morden Yolles; and others.

Spouse and colleague Molly Thom managed the interior design component and was encharged with procuring Trent's now-legendary furniture, which comprised original designs by Thom as well as selections from world-renowned designers. The College was designed to reflect and facilitate a different approach to higher education. In place of huge classrooms and lecture halls with separate buildings for student residences, Champlain would offer integration and intimacy. The student-to-teacher ratio would be very small, and instruction would take place in the faculty offices, common rooms and small seminar rooms—all within the same building that also would serve as the student dormitory. Wood-burning fireplaces, hand-made ceramics and beautiful crafted wooden furniture would reinforce the sense of warmth and communion

mixed with the concrete to allow the concrete to be pumped in. The steel forms were coated with retardant to delay the setting. When the forms were later stripped away, the concrete between stones was immediately scraped away by hand to expose the stone, which creates the wall's distinctive character.

throughout the College. The original concept would be short-lived, however. Partly due to cost pressures, and partly due to the subsequent regime's indifference to the original premise, a more conventional education delivery system would be adopted a few years after Trent's opening. Nonetheless, the utopian ideal resonated in full force in September 1964, as the first students were officially admitted to Trent University, which, as Symons declared, would present itself to the world as "a place of aesthetic as well as intellectual excitement." ▲

thomas symons

AFTERWORD:
RON THOM AT TRENT

RON THOM WAS, indeed, a genius—a creative genius in his ability to design and create things—buildings, furniture, and artefacts. But he was also a genius in terms of his conceptual thinking which is reflected in his work on the Master Plan for Trent University. He was a genius, too, in his care for and understanding of the needs and concerns of his clients. When the campus and buildings were being planned for Trent, I always asked him to sit with a working group of students and professors and Board members, and to listen to and participate in their discussions about the purpose and function of the building or project concerned, to learn first-hand from them what their aspirations were for that project or building—for what would go in it and for how it would work. This was basically the only instruction I ever gave Ron. It was a request, really, and he always faithfully observed it. He would listen

and join in, and then do his designs. The results were fabulous.

One fundamental point that emerged early in this process was that whatever was built or designed should show respect for the physical environment. I believe that the physical environment where educational activity occurs is a fundamental part of the educational experience and the opportunity that we provide to students. One of the aspects of a quality education is an understanding and appreciation of beauty and design. Ron Thom's entire campus is a wonderful example of this.

Ron Thom conceived the buildings of Trent to grow out of the landscape. They are not an imposition on the landscape, they are not an "add-on," and they are not hostile to the landscape. The buildings' relationship to one another and to the river—these aspects of the design

∨> Untitled watercolour renderings of Trent University,
Ron Thom, c. 1967. *Collection of the Canadian Architectural Archives at University of Calgary.*

mark them as *part* of the landscape. It's a superb
example of a conceptual architecture that is
respectful of the location.

Ron Thom also chose to use simple, good
materials in brilliant ways. His use of stone and
wood are extraordinary in their combination and
in the predominant note they strike. That, too, is
an expression of architecture that grows out of
its context rather than being imposed on it. The
concern was the relationship to the terrain in
which it sat, and Ron's buildings are wonderfully
in harmony with the river and with the hills that

immediately surround the buildings. I think it's
miraculous what he accomplished.

Some people have said that that the college
format at Trent is an idea that I picked up after
I received my University of Toronto scholarship
to Oxford University in England, but it is not. I
got the idea out of the old Canadian tradition of
colleges that goes back 200 years. You will find
such college structures at Dalhousie University
in Halifax, at the Universities of Saskatchewan,
Manitoba, Toronto, Western, and beyond. The
idea of having the smaller college community
as part of the larger unit of the university is one
of the oldest ideas in Canadian higher education, and one that I fear many Canadians have
forgotten about in an apparent rush to emulate
American institutions.

What academic leaders must do is put first
things first—and your first thing is your physical
presence: you either have a campus or you don't.
It's as simple as that. If you are lucky enough to
have a good one, don't fritter it away. Take stock
of what you have and, particularly if the campus
is already a masterpiece, be terribly careful with
what you do to it. The odds are high that you'll
muck it up, unless with whatever you do, you do
it respectfully for what has already been provided
by nature, or done well by humans.

There is a widespread delight in Ron's architecture. His private houses are full of surprises here and there: eyebrow windows, slot windows, and other features in unexpected places. Of his institutional projects, he has three gigantic masterpieces within Ontario: Massey College, the Shaw Theatre, and Trent University; and they're each functionally different in purpose and setting. His planning and architectural interpretation was just right for those three profoundly different settings: the heart of the biggest city; the small pioneer town; and an old Ontario small town. And what is miraculous is that it was all

news to him. He was a west-coast boy, and he had not yet had the chance to see the colleges of Cambridge and Oxford and Harvard. But what he did bring with him was respect for the setting: respect for nature and for the surrounding environment. At Trent this was combined with deep and thoughtful attention to the needs and concerns of the students and their professors.

It was an honour to know Ron Thom, and I enjoyed and valued everything we did together. He was a profoundly Canadian architect, and, I think, the greatest of our time. ▲

CONTRIBUTORS

TONY ROBINS is a recipient of the Canadian Prix de Rome in Architecture. He has a lively architecture and design practice in Vancouver, and is an Adjunct Professor of Architecture at the University of British Columbia, running an annual studio exploring architectural space. His student thesis was on the 20th-century history of appropriation and the effect of the media on the dissemination of architectural style. His writings have appeared in the Rizzoli monograph *Morphosis Architects* and in L'Architettura, Spain.

BRIGITTE SHIM, CM, BES, BArch, FRAIC, Hon. FAIA, RCA is a principal of Shim-Sutcliffe Architects and an Associate Professor at the John H. Daniels Faculty of Architecture, Landscape and Design. She was a founding member of the Bureau of Architecture and Urbanism. She and partner A. Howard Sutcliffe have been the College Architects for Massey College at the University of Toronto since 1995. Shim and Sutcliffe were both awarded the Order of Canada in 2013 "for their contributions as architects designing sophisticated structures that represent the best of Canadian design to the world."

THOMAS H.B. SYMONS, C.C., O.Ont., F.R.S.C., LL.D., D.U. D. Litt, D.Cn.L., F.R.G.S, K.S.S., is Founding President and Vanier Professor Emeritus of Trent University. He is the author and co-author of numerous articles, reports and books on international relations and Canadian history, culture, education, politics, and native rights, and has held presidencies in many organizations related to these topics. Professor Symons is Chair of the Ontario Heritage Trust and Past Chair of the Historic Sites and Monuments Board of Canada.

ADELE WEDER is a Vancouver-based architectural writer and the curator of *Ron Thom and the Allied Arts*. Her master's thesis focused on the architecture of B.C. Binning, and she co-authored the Douglas & McIntyre monograph *B.C. Binning* in 2006. She is co-author and editor of *Selwyn Pullan: Positioning the New* and a contributing essayist to several other books and monographs. A correspondent for design publications in North America and abroad, she received the 2011 President's Award for Architectural Journalism from RAIC/Architecture Canada.

ACKNOWLEDGEMENTS

A GREAT MANY individuals and organizations have been instrumental in bringing this project to fruition. We are wholly indebted to Shanna Fromson, who provided the bedrock support for the production of this catalogue.

We extend special thanks to Lee Hays, Richard Morgan, Jodi Aoki and Thomas Symons of Trent University; Amela Marin, P.J. MacDougall and John Fraser of Massey College; Linda Fraser and Dave Brown of the Canadian Architectural Archives at University of Calgary; Kiriko Watanabe and other staff at the West Vancouver Museum. We are grateful to architectural photographers Steven Evans, John Flanders, Selwyn Pullan and the late Peter Varley; and to essayists Tony Robins, Brigitte Shim and Thomas Symons. Public: Architecture + Communication has created an exceptional design for the exhibition at the heart of this catalogue. Ron Thom's family members—Robin, Sydney, Bronwen, Aaron and Chris; Adam, Emma and Molly—have served as exceptional sources of information, artefacts and support. Barry Downs, Paul Merrick, Paul Martel, Paul Barnard, Alastair Grant and Dick-Sai-Chew are among the many former colleagues who have been helpful, as have former clients Geoffrey Massey, Dr. Morton and Irene Dodek, the D.H. Copp family, and the late Murray Frum. Nancy Lockhart, Rob Tuckerman, Jan Pidhirny, Jim Ferguson, Ed and Edlyn Pattyn, Brigitte Desrochers, Josh Nychuk and Jacob Hiltz have all made important contributions. Helena Grdadolnik of Workshop Architecture, Rachel Gotlieb of the Gardiner Museum, John Leroux and Terry Graff of the Beaverbrook Art Gallery have helped bring the project to Ontario and beyond. Graphic designer Jessica Sullivan has done masterful work in creating this catalogue. We are appreciative of the early support and encouragement from RAIC/Architecture Canada, DIALOG, Toronto Society of Architects and Ontario Association of Architects. We thank all supporters for whom the limits of time or space preclude their naming here. We are deeply grateful to the Canada Council for the Arts and the British Columbia Arts Council for supporting the exhibition that feeds the contents of these pages.

DARRIN MORRISON ▲ ADELE WEDER

*for Daphne Harris, the glue that held
the office together; and for the unsung
heroes of the creative process*

WEST VANCOUVER MUSEUM
www.westvancouvermuseum.ca

Front cover: *Top* Champlain College, Trent University, Peterborough (detail, cropped). Photo: Steven
Evans. *Centre* Massey College, Toronto (detail, cropped). Photo: Peter Varley. *Bottom* Forrest House,
West Vancouver (detail, cropped). Photo: Selwyn Pullan. Back cover: *Top* Champlain College dining
hall, Trent University (detail, cropped). Photo: Steven Evans. *Centre* Massey College dining hall
(detail, cropped). Photo: Peter Varley. *Bottom* Forrest House, interior (detail, cropped). Photo: Selwyn
Pullan. Frontispiece: Reginald Faryon Bridge (underside), c. 1969, by Ron Thom, Paul Merrick,
Morden Yolles and Roly Bergmann, Trent University. Photo: Steven Evans.

Edited by Adele Weder
Design by Jessica Sullivan
Printed and bound in Canada by Hemlock Printers

Library and Archives Canada Cataloguing in Publication
Ron Thom and the allied arts / [essays by] Tony Robins, Brigitte Shim,
Thomas Symons; edited by Adele Weder.
A catalogue of a traveling exhibition held at the West Vancouver Museum on July 4
to September 21, 2013, and at the Gardiner Museum, in Toronto from February 4
to May 7, 2014, and at Trent University from August 7 to October 22, 2014.

ISBN 978-0-9919602-1-7 (pbk.)

1. Thom, Ron—Exhibitions. I. Symons, T.H.B. (Thomas Henry Bull), 1929–, writer of added
commentary II. Shim, Brigitte, 1958–, writer of added commentary III. Weder, Adele, 1961–,
writer of added commentary, editor of compilation IV. Robins, Tony, 1952–, writer of added
commentary V. West Vancouver Museum issuing body, host institution
NA749.T48A4 2013   720.92   C2013-905338-7

ISBN 978-0-9919602-1-7

9 780991 960217